Pieces of Her Storms and Sunshines

Jenny Rae Tillery

BookLeaf Publishing

Presentation by *BookLeaf Publishing*

Web: www.bookleafpub.com

E-mail: info@bookleafpub.com

ISBN: 9789357214384

First edition 2023

I dedicate this book to all my littles. The hundreds of children that I never gave birth to but love you just as I did. If I could stage this world to never break your heart, you know that I would. Although I can't take away the pains of life, I want to leave you with something to remember. The Sun will ALWAYS shine after that storm. Sometimes we just need the rain to clear the path and our vision :). I love you #MORE.

Special dedication to Jonathon, Austin, Kaylin, Westlyn, Oaklyn, and my Fairy Goddaughter.... Kayleigh Elizabeth....... I pray that you know how deep my love for you flows ♡.

ACKNOWLEDGEMENT

First, I must give all the Glory to God. Jesus brought me out of my grave and he carries me daily, so I will forever sing his praises. Next, there is my loving mother, Lynnie. God gave me you and there is not a doubt about that. Thank you for not only believing in me, but for supporting me in every dream, idea, and crazy thing I ever decided I wanted to chase after. I will always know that you are my biggest fan! You are my rock! Then, there is my husband.... Jeremiah. There is love.... my love, and then... there is us.... destined to love.... Jeremiah and Jennifer. You are the very beat to my heart. You are my person, my strength. I believe I may not be alive had it not been for your love, patience, understanding... and stubbornness. I thank God twice daily for you. Next, is my close circle of sisters and brothers in Christ. You have lifted me up during the hardest times. You breathed life into my dry bones, and I would be lost without you. "A sweet friendship refreshes the soul" - Proverbs 27:9 (The Holy Bible). To my family and friends. I have been encouraged daily by each of you.... I love you dearly. Please believe that a compliment or positive word can change a life. It lifts us up. Last, but not least...... there are those that don't like me and even oppose me. Those that refused, neglected me, and turned their back on me. Those that have torn me down, abused me, deceived me, lied to me and about me. The ones that hurt me. I say to you sincerely... I am praying to see you do well. I forgive you. Forgiveness does not have to partner with reconciliation. In a small way, you built me up too. So, I acknowledge that you inspired me to not quit or give up. I bless thee. I am just humbly thankful for this opportunity!

PREFACE

The writings in this poetic collection come from my life experiences. They highlight some of my darkest struggles and most precious memories as well! I have always heard writings, music, and movie scripts are most highly impacted by love or heartache. In my experience, this is true. It is those deep emotions that produce the passion of art.

I have been drafting stories, poems, quotes, and thoughts since I could form my Three-year-old hand to hold a writing instrument. It was my intention to choose a variety of my works in different topic areas. Love, heartache, worship, nature, family, and life lessons are my most influential subjects. I carefully chose each poem in hopes of reaching a broad audience. I am aware that this book may not be everyone's cup of tea, however I hope that each reader takes some time to explore the different topics throughout the book. As humans, we all have passions just as we all have felt pain. My goals are to share my story, of the storms and the struggles, but most importantly of the good stuff and the healing too. I hope to inspire every reader that no matter what you are currently facing, you are strong, and there IS.... sunshine after the storm!

A Poem for My Mother

A Poem for My Mother

Written November 19, 2019

If roses are red, and violets are blue,

I have some things to say to you.

I want you to know just what you mean to me,

I'd like you to look through my eyes and see what I see.

From my earliest memories and every day since then,

You have been the best mother for me that God could have sent.

There are mothers that cook, clean and wash your hair.

There are mothers that hold you tight when a dream gives you a scare.

There are mothers that teach you to read and write;

There are mothers that try everything just to get through the night.

Some mothers have it easy with lots of money and a loving Dad.

You weren't that mother, but you gave it all you had.

Even if we had it, that wouldn't have changed our past.

Yet still you taught me all I know, gave me plenty of love to last.

Life was never easy for us; we are too stubborn for that.

We wouldn't have succeeded without falling flat.

If getting back up was an art, we made experts long ago.

I wouldn't change a thing; we are wiser in what we know.

MOMMY… I love you, you are my very best friend,

someone I can trust, my partner until the end!

Looking back on our life, things may have been a mess,

but you are the best part… to this I confess.

You turned me into a lady with a heart forever pure;

showed me grace and kindness out of this world.

Not just on your birthday but every day after that,

I want you to know I love you and will always have your back.

Happy Birthday Mommy,

With love always,

Your Babygirl,

JENNIFER RAE

A Kiss

A Kiss

Written August 18, 2015

A kiss can say many things, without a word being spoken.

It can give you a hundred highs or be worth more than a token.

A kiss can say "I know you", "I miss you when you're gone".

A kiss can say "I love you", "I think of you when I'm alone".

A kiss can be like glitter, at least.... a sparkling bliss,

A kiss makes your heart beat faster, so nervous you nearly miss.

A kiss can pick you up, make you feel like you have wings.

A kiss can hold you down, put your mind at ease.

A kiss can give you tingles, in all the right places.

A kiss can combine the lips of two loving faces.

A kiss can say “Hey! Look what you do to me”,

Or stop you in your tracks... say “forever be true to me”.

A kiss can be soft and taste perfectly sweet.

A kiss can pick you up when you are feeling weak.

A kiss can say “Hello!” and a kiss can say “Good-bye”.

A kiss can say “I’m sorry” or a kiss can say “I tried”.

A kiss can say everything, if you open up your heart.

A kiss can be perfect from the very start.

Some kisses are a secret, only meant for me and you.

Others are for crowds, when the owners say I do.

First kisses are precious, they only happen one time.

They steal a heart away, the way that you stole mine.

Some kisses are sneaky, hidden in a room.

If the others find out, who knows what they would do.

A kiss can be casual or filled with passion too!

But the best kisses come from my lips and press themselves to you.

Our kisses are like magic, and you know I tell the truth.

Sweeter than cherries and just as soft too!

So, when it comes to kisses.... not just ANY kiss will do,

I only want the forever I feel when I kiss you!

My Little Love

My Little Love

Written December 11, 2022

For Kaylin, Kayleigh, and all my Littles!

My little love... you are so precious.
My little love... you are so rare.
You're beauty mesmerizes me,
I can't control my stare.

When you are deep in your thoughts,
Or playing with your toys,
I inspect your routines,
You fill me with joy!

I am not your mother,

And I can't see you every day,

Yet I'm pleased to have you in my life,

And I always hope you stay.

Because...

My little love... you are so precious.

You bring a smile to my face.

You tread on my heart heavily;

I keep you in a special place!

I love to read you stories and teach you everything that I can.

We play with games and toys; I take you on trips I love to plan.

From watching cartoons to shopping, and fun festivities too,

My days are so much sweeter, When I get to spend time with you.

My little love... you are so precious.

More than you may know,

It melts my heart to leave you,

When you have to go.

Take your time my little baby, don't rush through life so fast.

I don't want to miss this moment; I want these memories to last.

In the blink of an eye, you will get older and have Littles of your own,

There won't be much time to visit, or to call me on the phone.

So, take it easy my little love, Let's enjoy these moments we are in.

Because once we get to those days, we can't come back here again.

My little love... you are so precious.

Even when you are all grown...

You will always be My little love....

And I will love your Littles as my own!

A Million Tears

A Million Tears

Written around 2003

Finished near the end of September 2016

I feel I've cried a million tears,

enough to flood God's earth.

I know I've wallowed in my pain,

repeated cycles of losing my worth.

I searched the world high and low,

in hopes of finding love and grace.

I found it here or there,

but always end up back in the same place.

Oh, how the cycles of addiction have plagued
this pretty face.

My face can be painted up,

these tears, they wipe away.

Yet this heart carries so many burdens...

it pushes everyone astray.

I don’t want to be lonely,

although I feel it every day.

I just pray for a storm big enough

to blow the past away.

I must have cried a million tears,

enough to put out the sun.

I have wallowed in my agony...

and prayed this pain be done.

The Cold

The Cold

Written around 2009

For the death and loss of my brother, Dusty.

Winter.

The cold took him.

He left without a goodbye.

My heart will always ache for him.

I cry.

My tears,

They fall so slow.

I will never forget.

The pain will always remain here.

I’m cold.

Scars That Remain

Scars That Remain

Written May 10, 2015

Love can be a dangerous game that we play...

when someone attractive smiles and looks our way.

Butterflies, tingles, and a fast-beating heart...

suddenly, nothing could ever keep you apart.

As feelings grow stronger and emotions get deeper,

reality sets in… that you won't do anything it takes to keep her.

Begging and pleading can't change your mind,

when poison in a bottle occupies all your time.

Hearts get battered, shattered and broken;

Venomous words get spit and spoken.

Liquid crystals stream down her soft face;

She knows there's no way she can keep up at
this pace.

She begged you for years... through all her tears,

letting go now feels…. less like a fear.

You slip from her grasp; she has fewer reasons
to fight.

She's tired of the battles she fights alone day and
night.

She closes her eyes once more as her vision
begins to rain.

She welcomes in the hope of a better day... one
without all this pain.

But all that's left now…. are the scars that
remain.

Always Be Here

Always Be Here

Written November 27, 2017; For my husband….Jeremiah.
(Side Note: The next few poems express our relationship love
and struggles during the course of Jeremiah's incarceration.)

Sometimes in life, things can feel a bit unfair.

Looking at what you don't have could put your heart in despair.

Now I'm not being hasty, I know I'm blessed to the core.

Yet there are some things in life that I'd like to have a little more.

What I would give at the first daylight rays,

to open my eyes and see your handsome face.

To feel the warmth of your body on these cold winter days;

To spend our summers chasing waves on all these local beach bays.

What I would do, just to be able to feel……

your fingertips dance on my skin as I lay super still.

To taste the sweetness from your sexy soft lips,

or enjoy the love making with our grinding hips.

I'm not talking crazy; this is how I really feel.

The bond between us is unbreakable and real.

Sometimes the crave and wait; they are just so hard,

but I will never let them push or pull us apart.

For even with all I want and would love to do with you,

this thing we have right now, is super special too.

I wouldn't give it up, not for anything at all;

my heart beats twice when I see your call.

Your voice soothes my mind, puts my soul at ease.

We talk about everything from the A's to the Z's.

When I am sad, you put a smile on my face.

You comfort me with love; it feels like I'm floating in space.

When I am being difficult, you throw tough love my way.

You even listen to my complaining when I had a horrible day.

The purpose of these words is to show you that I care,

to tell you that I love you, and I will always be here!

Love always,

Jenny Rae Sunshine

Almost

Almost

Written for Jeremiah on January 13, 2020

I almost woke to your whisper when I was deep in a sleep.

Almost felt that heartbeat, saw your eyes open a little peek.

I almost tasted your kiss, with a sweet tongue tango.

Almost gazed a picnic in a field, soaking up rays and snacking on mangos.

I almost had a memory of your fingers giving my hair a tangle.

I was almost blinded by the sun, reflecting off your dimple.

You were beside me in my car…. at just the right angle.

I almost caught a shiver, as your warm breath hit my shoulder,

Almost had a distant memory of us together growing older.

I almost felt my hand in yours with my afternoon walk.

I almost listened to us stay up all night… just to giggle and talk.

I almost tasted your cooking. I had my breakfast in bed.

You had my coffee in your hands, pressed your lips to my forehead.

I almost ran back inside, just before I left for the day.

I had to squeeze you again, in your love I'm always safe.

I almost called you at lunchtime, or anytime that I wanted.

Almost watched you check all the rooms when I thought the house felt haunted.

I almost got my foot rub…. at the end of a hard workday,

Almost got a bubble bath too... almost loved the pain away.

I almost fell asleep on your chest, cuddled in for the night.

Almost felt your arms holding me just right.

I almost stayed in our dreams, just a little happy zone.

Almost caught wind of your scent, it was better than cologne.

I almost messed up a good thing, it was hard to smile through the pain.

Almost lost my control… when you mailed me that ring.

I almost gave up a few times…. this life ain't for the weak.

Almost got caught a few times too, felt the adrenaline in the sneak.

I almost know we are getting closer; I feel it deep down in my heart.

Almost get to live our life together, no more apart.

I almost feel the tears, crazy pumping in my heart!

I almost can't swallow, feel the excitement from the thought!

I almost can't stand it, but we are on God's time now.

He will mold us into his plan, strengthen us and teach us how.

I almost fell in love… well, that's almost true….

Jeremiah, there is no almost... I completely love you!

Lasting Lovers

Lasting Lovers

Written for Jeremiah May 18, 2020

(Department of Corrections visitation was closed

for over 2 months due to COVID-19 Pandemic)

Lasting Lovers, that's something rare to have in this time.

No one holds on, they're only there for a thrill ride.

When the struggle rises, they slip off into the night.

No effort to help with your needs, to them you aren't worth the fight.

Tough times don't last, but tough people do.

I found my strength when I laid eyes on you.

Lasting lovers... we had no clue,

that our hearts would connect and carry us right through.

This journey we walk is rougher than many others,

But we will pass right through, we're lasting lovers.

Society talks against us, feels like we're fighting a losing battle,

But we got each other's backs and that's the only thing that matters.

Lasting Lovers, slaying all the demons life sends our way.

But we hold each other tight, until we see the light of better days.

Even in the darkest hours, when we feel like giving in,

We remember what we have and throw the world a spin.

Time feels so slow when we can't talk or touch or kiss,

just hang in there baby; our future's filled with bliss.

I know the distance shakes you; trust that I feel this heartache too,

but we are lasting lovers, our bond will heal us through.

So, when the night takes over and you're cold, sad, and blue,

close your eyes and feel your heartbeat, remember that's my heart too.

Feel my chicken noodle soup hugs, taste the sugars from my kiss,

Let my love protect you, don't focus on the miss.

Every storm runs out of rain, and this storm will pass us too,

Because we are lasting lovers…. Forever Forevers... just me and you!

What Is Love

What Is Love

Written for Jeremiah January 09, 2019

What is love….

But an expression from the heart…

It is the melody heard in music,

The colors viewed in art.

What is love….

But a feeling….

Something expressed through a deep care.

It's invisible,

Yet the presence floats through the air.

Love is Rare and Precious,

One of the most prized possessions of life.

It's the smell of a newborn baby,

The glitter in newlyweds' eyes.

What is love……. Is a great question.

The answer is so complex.

Love surpasses everything, worth more than money,

More pleasurable than sex.

Love is highly craved.

Wanted by most... it wears the fame.

But when things go horribly wrong,

It is love that takes the blame.

Some people swear off love; they never again want to hear the word.

Too many times in life.... their hearts were broken and burned.

Dealing with that heartache, was a lesson not easily learned.

What is love…. We wonder often times,

when it leaves us all alone with tears flowing from our eyes.

The happiness we thought we knew ended in betrayal and lies.

For as awesome as love can make us feel... when that sweetness fades to sour,

The pain and sorrow are too real, we hide in our sadness for countless hours.

What is love….

That is the question that carries on through the years.

Some are drawn to it like a magnet, others rush away to disappear.

I was one of those lovers, left high and dry from heartache's bite.

Laying on the cold dark floor, inside me there was no remaining fight.

What is love….

Now... I will never have to ask myself; You made it very clear.

You put my broken pieces back together and healed every tear!

Love is what we have right here... a direct path from your heart to mine.

It's in our breath, our very being, and it just gets sweeter with time.

What is love….

We never have to ask; we have felt it for a thousand lives.

For as long as there is existence, our souls will always align.

What is love….

You ask, my dear? The answer is as sweet as wine.

Love is what we feel when your heart connects with mine.

We are love…… Jeremiah

I love you today. I love you tomorrow. I love you always.

I love you a thousand lifetimes and then more....

Your Love Taught Me How

Your Love Taught Me How

Written July 2021

Inspired by Amirah's writing

Some people say there's no such thing as
Forever… Fairy-tale Love.

Your love taught me different.

Many others think that a love like that means
peachy perfect….

with all rainbows and unicorns, sparkling
cupcakes too.

Your love showed me that was also not true.

Once, I was naive in my views of love,

Thinking one sided and assuming so much.

Your love taught me to humble myself,

See another's perspective and such.

Your love came on strong… there was no denying it,

came in like an angel just when I had lost faith in it.

Your love taught me to wait on it.

I've loved a few before, ended up despising it.

Lost hope in having a companion and partner to do this life with.

Your love taught me to hold on.

Trying to put words to this magical bond we have,

is like trying to implement a multi- dimensional idea to a one planed surface….

It just doesn't make sense.

And your love taught me that sometimes love doesn't make sense.

Your love taught me to hang on when I wanted to give up.

It taught me to sit down and shut up because this ride can get rough.

Your love is fierce. Your love is bold.

Taught me how hang on, and when to let go.

You taught me to look in the mirror and how much power I have,

You taught me to look into my own eyes and see the blessing I am.

Your love taught me self-love,

Something I only thought I had.

You taught me you can love someone,

And still be fire mad.

You taught me love can make you laugh,

Even when your day can be so sad,

You taught me how to fight for our love, with everything I have.

You showed me the way, to help myself change.

You supported me through transitions, I never would have made.

One promise changed it all.....

We never walk away.

Words come cheap, living in these days.

Your love taught me to look at my own actions,

You forced me to hold myself to higher standards.

I didn't know how to change myself, yet you never left me stranded.

Your love taught me the way.

You taught me kindness and a mercy that I had never faced.

You taught me undying forgiveness with a splash of grace.

Love does hurt, only as you grow and learn.

We not hitting each other or throwing daggers with our words.

This is about building each other up, making smiles out of our faces.

Hugging and kissing, finding beauty in all places.

Your love taught me to smile.

And I don't mean just the one on our faces.

You taught me the heart repairs,

When given time, love, and space.

Love is like life, it's the journey that matters,

Not so much the ending.

Your love shows me every day,

True Love was worth the finding.

Your love has lifted me up,

We're floating together now.

I am learning to enjoy the moment

And I'm so glad... your love taught me how.

Jaded by the Stain

Jaded by the Stain

Written July 2021

One look at your photo. Lust crept in like smoldering smoke.

What's a few letters, some flirting, and jokes.

It didn't take us long to discover, our connection wouldn't easily severe.

Just coasting along… we really had no clue.

I felt not to trust you, but my eyes were confused.

The lonely heart can be ruthless, this statement bleeds true,

My own heart deceived me, I thought I wanted you.

I always fell weak… for a smart guy with a pretty face.

Looking back now… I feel dishonored and disgraced….

And Jaded by the Stain you left on my heart.

Against my own logic, and everything I had learned…

I let you set me on fire… and I willingly burned.

I betrayed my soul, and ripped out my own heart…

I battled my intuition…. and allowed you the leading part.

Just two characters in some altered reality.

I let you march right in and partially devour me.

No. I was no saint, you clearly got me there.

I grasped on tighter with my intentions and thirst for your love and care.

“Behaviors don’t lie” ... to that quote I do swear.

When your actions changed, I knew this love was not rare.

Once I opened up my eyes, the truth unraveled there.

Everything was exposed so quickly; I was not prepared.

I prayed for clarity, for God to take my pain.

I asked forgiveness… washed clean like the rain.

The Holy King has mercy, my learned lessons will remain.

Even though I'm left Jaded by this Heart that carries your stain.

Blessed I am to know … that love covers a multitude of sin.

Forgiveness will heal me. My true love comes from within.

But first there will be aching, tears streaming to my chin.

I remember that after the storm, the sun always shines again!

She Sat with It

She Sat with It

Written August 15, 2022

She sat with it.

Still .... in the movements.

Quiet… in the chaos.

She merely observed.

She thought on it.

Her tears were there,

Yet no longer was her face wet.

The silent tears just added extra weight to her heart.

She sat through it.

Thinking over every little detail.

Lost but somehow figuring out her way.

She analyzed from the beginning to where she was now.

She pondered the memories.

She made sense of the series of unfortunate events.

Never had she been so still.

Rolling through the settings in her mind like a movie reel.

She calculated the formulas.

Made rise of those things she had overlooked before.

She pieced it all together.

She ached on it.

Wishing she had realized oh so much sooner.

Quiet and unwavering … she posed.

As if a dolly, yes. Waiting on the shelf.

She rebutted her findings.

Cross referenced it all.

Now Wishing she hadn't figured it out.

But once she knew, she couldn't unknow.

So, she sat with it some more.

She felt it.

Deeply.

Like a lightning bolt, she was immediately aware.

More so than ever.

She wanted to run, hide, or disappear.

Wanted to go back to a time before.

Couldn't see a glimmer of any lights ahead.

Didn't know the path she should pursue now.

She waded through.

Had no way to escape these truths.

Found no words to make things new.

So steady as a rock....

She sat with it.

That Silent Heartbreak

That Silent Heartbreak

Written November 7, 2022

Inspired by Renee (and my own heartbreaks too)
- Sister, when you hurt…… I hurt too.

That silent Heartbreak

The one no one sees.

Words never speak it,

We keep it internally.

I'm not supposed to love you.

I no longer should care.

I shouldn't torture myself

With the memories we shared.

I need to let go, move on,

Just like you did, I guess.

But …. How can I do that

When my existence was made a mess.

I need to give it time,

That's what everyone would say.

But… how can I reach tomorrow,

When I'm struggling with today.

So…. that silent heartbreak,

I tuck it a little deeper.

It tears my world apart;

I thought you were a keeper.

True love, forever,

Happily ever after,

These thoughts cut me like a sword,

Snatch me up like the rapture.

I don't want to see your face,

Can't stand to hear your name.

I don't want to feel these memories,

All they carry now is pain.

That silent heartbreak...

It's all that I have now.

Still.... I must paint my courage,

Face the world somehow.

We all fall down,

Get back up they speak.

My body feels the shaking,

My spirit remains so weak.

As the darkness of another lonely night

Starts to creep back in... I wonder...

How will I ever find myself again?

Forbidden but Fruitful

Forbidden but Fruitful

Do you desire me…. crave me?

Do thoughts of my taste … fast forward and then rewind?

Does my existence pose intensity through your flesh and mind?

Is it sweet like cherries... or does it spank your tongue like a pepper?

Does it dominate your thoughts and is fighting it …. somehow a disaster?

Forbidden fruit .... enticing.... your heartbeats a little faster.

Resisting you is an art that I haven't quite mastered.

Heat rushes through my veins; I pray it moves faster.

My little miss river flows; I just can't catch her.

It feels so pleasing... I know just what I'm after.

Light biting, candle wax and a tongue to outlast her.

Fingertips, body sweat, and a kiss to seal our fate.

There's a heavy price on my sins but I just can't negotiate.

White flag waving, I succumb to misbehaving.

I want to be good but can no longer beat this craving.

The only thing between us is a metal fence and time waiting.

Not knowing for sure if our fantasies are debating.

Wanting you so bad my body goes into shaking.

I wonder if it's just me or what your thoughts are saying.

I keep it mostly in, for the heart I am betraying.

In another lifetime, another realm.... we could be slaying.

Barefoot in the country simple life playing.

Imagination keeps us held, it's the only world we're safe in.

Because the truth that we feel, we must keep our lips from saying.

No matter what, I'm here, my passion I'm displaying.

No word can really describe this situation we stay in.

But I'm along for the ride, just keep the sun beams racing.

We both have something to give, and we both enjoy the taking.

Not sure where it leads but we can accept no faking.

So, we enjoy the connection, try not to get too deep in.

Learning and feeling... that is the destination.

I want to leave you with my message,

Hope I make an impression.

You leave a mark on my mind

And touch a piece of my heart too.

When you hear my name,

I hope it brings happiness through.

The way you get inside my thoughts

And put a smile on me too.

Something Had to Give

Something Had to Give

I already miss the kiss

That I never got to taste.

All those dreams and fantasies….

Just a mental waste.

My heart still aches so real...

It's more than I can take.

Been all around this situation…

To end up back in the same place.

Something had to give,

Someone had to break.

I guess... I was hoping...

The choice would somehow fade.

Now I lay here broken,

Tears flowing…. in the bed I made.

When the dust settles,

And the storm clouds roll away;

I pray I brought you more pleasure

And the pain doesn't stay.

They say it is better to love and lose,

Than to never love at all….

I pray your future has happiness,

And all over you the blessings fall.

Healing for the Pain

Healing for the Pain

Written May 30, 2022

People will hurt you.

People will hurt you.

People will hurt you.

People will hurt God.

You will hurt people.

You will hurt God.

God heals.

God heals.

God heals.

Amen ♡♡♡

The Fall Down

The Fall Down

Written March 06, 2022

There is an equal amount of joy to be perceived…

from the watching of a leaf that glides down...

to the ground with a twist and whirl dance;

In a slow breeze at the change of a season,

As there is to catch the moment in time…

In the night sky,

Gazing the release and willful fall and fade out

Of a beautifully lit shining diamond star.

The fall down is important.

Not quite so as the rise up, but just as critical.

For in the vulnerability of our fall, during that lowest of low moments,

that's what makes us.

That is the pinpointed location in life…

that we chose to claim victorious over anything opposing our healing,

and the divine plan.

If not for that moment…

that fall down part;

There would be nowhere to rise from.

So, fall. Fall down…. my love.

Fall all the way down.

Then take a moment.

Take just enough time,

to catch your breath.

Arm yourself with the weapons of your faith…

and rest.

Then you go to battle.

Make the choices it takes to rise up…

to stay focused,

to get and stay well.

Get closer to God.

Talk to him daily.

Read his word.

Worship him like the superstar you were designed to be.

Fellowship with accountable and anointed sisters and brothers.

Plead out his grace on your life.

Put that crown of royalty back on your head….

and take your place in the kingdom.

Then …. NEVER look back.

Keep your eyes focused above,

and God will heal the rest!

Then smile…. my love.

Your most genuinely glamorous smile!

Be happy.

Know now, that God has you in His Presence.

Don’t Forget to Smile

Don’t Forget to Smile

Written September 15, 2022

For Tiffany… and the others we have lost too soon.

Don’t forget to smile...

My friend…. I leave you with these words.

I know your hearts are heavy,

But for me…. I made it through the worst.

Life is but a moment....

We pass right through this earthly place.

Love and joy are important,

So don’t let sadness take up too much space.

Don’t forget to smile.

I miss you all to pieces,

And I love you even more.

That’s why I want to see you happy….

Even as the rain begins to pour.

Don’t forget to smile.

Sure, we have our troubles.

They will come and they will go.

But when you get those moments,

There’s something you need to know.

Don't forget to smile.

Even in those faith shaking storms.

Your spirit will get weary,

Your hearts, they may be worn.

For me, I'm up here dancing.

I'm singing with the band.

Resting in His Presence,

Someday you will understand.

But until that time is upon you,

Please do one thing I ask.

I know it may seem difficult,

But it's such a beautiful task.

Don't forget to smile.

Don't forget to smile.

Even if some tears fall down.

Listen for the trumpets,

They're playing my sound.

When you make it to Heaven,

I will meet you at the gates.

And we can smile together,

As we embrace our new fates.

Don’t forget to smile.

For now... I’m in the Kingdom,

As blissful as can be.

I’m finally with our father….

So don’t forget to smile for me.

Cry by the Water

Cry by the Water

Written March 5, 2022

Cry by the water,

Just let those streams flow down.

Don't worry how it looks,

Scream out your painful sound.

The best time is in solace,

With no one else around,

Only then can you release the truth,

And healing soon will be found.

Cry by the water.

It's the best place to let it all go.

There's something about Earth's water,

It seems to dwell in the know.

Sitting by the shore or maybe submerged
inside...

Take captive of those sorrows,

Then send them on their parting ride.

Cry by the water...

Let Jesus wipe away the tears for you.

Cry by the water...

Allow God to conquer your fears too.

Cry by the water,

Because if you only knew...

There will be many days ahead....

That you will...

Laugh and smile by the waters too!

Find Me by the Riverside

Find Me by the Riverside

Written in the Summer 2020

Through sunshine and storms,

You can find me by the riverside.

I'm learning deeply why I love this place;

It fills my soul with God's grace.

When we are feeling alone…

He creates the breeze that touches our face.

He feeds the river to run a steady pace.

The sounds of the water flowing...

Always give my heart a race.

The presence of true love,

It resets me to home base.

I look up at the sky,

His clouds... they comfort.

What a beautiful space.

The birds soar above;

The crickets make some calls,

Mullet fish are hopping,

No blessing is too small!

Two best friend flowers...

Sunbathe on the shore.

They show strength amongst all the weeds,

And add beauty even more.

Jesus thank you for this life,

You give me all the love I need.

I will forever sing your praises…

And witness to your good deeds.

You bring water to the valleys,

And sunshine to the sky.

Now and for always… I exalt you,

With my hands raised way up high!

Hallelujah!

www.ingramcontent.com/pod-product-compliance
Lightning Source LLC
Chambersburg PA
CBHW051734130826
49812CB00033B/854
9789357214384